Cuttlefish

by Colleen Sexton

BELLWETHER MEDIA · MINNEAPOLIS, MN

Note to Librarians, Teachers, and Parents:

Blastoff! Readers are carefully developed by literacy experts and combine standards-based content with developmentally appropriate text.

Level 1 provides the most support through repetition of high-frequency words, light text, predictable sentence patterns, and strong visual support.

Level 2 offers early readers a bit more challenge through varied simple sentences, increased text load, and less repetition of high-frequency words.

Level 3 advances early-fluent readers toward fluency through increased text and concept load, less reliance on visuals, longer sentences, and more literary language.

Level 4 builds reading stamina by providing more text per page, increased use of punctuation, greater variation in sentence patterns, and increasingly challenging vocabulary.

Level 5 encourages children to move from "learning to read" to "reading to learn" by providing even more text, varied writing styles, and less familiar topics.

Whichever book is right for your reader, Blastoff! Readers are the perfect books to build confidence and encourage a love of reading that will last a lifetime!

This edition first published in 2010 by Bellwether Media, Inc.

No part of this publication may be reproduced in whole or in part without written permission of the publisher. For information regarding permission, write to Bellwether Media, Inc., Attention: Permissions Department, 5357 Penn Avenue South, Minneapolis, MN 55419.

Library of Congress Cataloging-in-Publication Data
Sexton, Colleen A., 1967-
   Cuttlefish / by Colleen Sexton.
      p. cm. – (Blastoff! readers. Oceans alive)
   Includes bibliographical references and index.
   Summary: "Simple text and full-color photographs introduce beginning readers to cuttlefish. Developed by literacy experts for students in kindergarten through third grade"–Provided by publisher.
   ISBN 978-1-60014-273-4 (hardcover : alk. paper)
   1. Cuttlefish–Juvenile literature. I. Title.

QL430.3.S47S49 2010
594.58–dc22   2009008185

Printed in the United States of America, North Mankato, MN.   110110   1178

Contents

Cuttlefish are **mollusks**.
Mollusks are a group of animals
that have no backbone.

4

Cuttlefish live in warm, shallow areas of the ocean. They stay close to the ocean floor.

Cuttlefish come in many sizes.
The smallest cuttlefish are the size
of your big toe.

Some cuttlefish are as long as you are!

A cuttlefish has a soft, oval-shaped body. A thick, flat shell called a **cuttlebone** is inside its body.

The cuttlebone has empty spaces inside of it. Cuttlefish fill the spaces with water to dive.

Cuttlefish have big eyes that help them see in dark places.

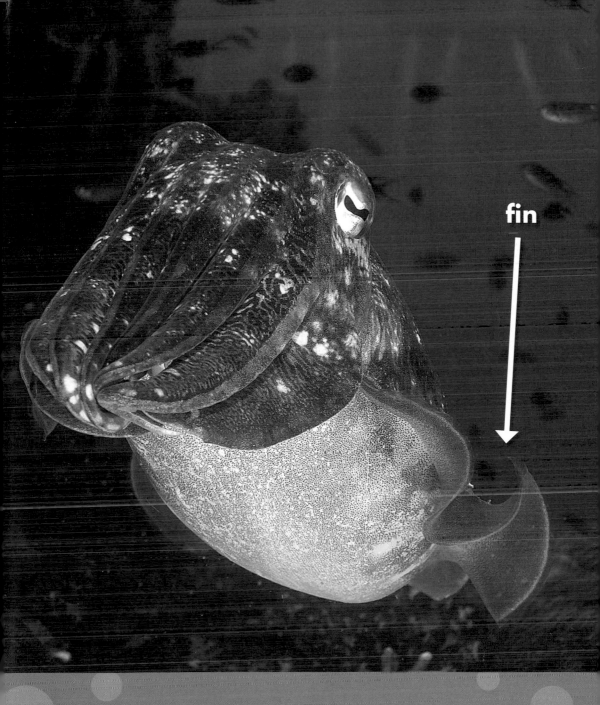

fin

A cuttlefish has a strong **fin**.
The fin helps it swim forward,
backward, and sideways.

funnel

Each cuttlefish has a **funnel**.
This long, hollow muscle helps
a cuttlefish swim fast.

A cuttlefish lets water into its body. Then it squeezes water out through its funnel to jet away.

tentacles

Each cuttlefish has two long **tentacles**. The tentacles tuck inside pockets near the eyes.

14

Cuttlefish shoot out their
tentacles to grab fish, clams,
and other **prey**.

prey

Eight arms surround the mouth of a cuttlefish. Each arm has **suckers** for holding on to prey.

16

suckers

beak

A cuttlefish has a sharp **beak** for a mouth. The beak tears apart prey.

Cuttlefish can change shape and color to match their surroundings. This is called **camouflage**.

Cuttlefish use camouflage to hide from sharks, dolphins, and other **predators**.

Cuttlefish have another way to escape predators. They squirt out a cloud of ink.

The ink surprises predators.
Whoosh! The cuttlefish swims
away!

Glossary

beak—the hard part of the mouth that helps a cuttlefish eat food

camouflage—the blending of an animal into its surroundings when it changes color, shape, or size

cuttlebone—the hard, bony shell inside a cuttlefish that helps it float or sink in the water

fins—the parts of an ocean animal used to move, steer, and stop in the water; cuttlefish only have one fin.

funnel—a strong muscle shaped like a tube that helps cuttlefish move in the water

mollusk—a group of animals that have a soft body and no backbone; some mollusks have shells; snails, clams, and octopuses are examples of mollusks.

predator—an animal that hunts other animals for food

prey—an animal that is hunted by another animal for food

suckers—the round, cup-shaped parts on a cuttlefish's arms; suckers can bend and stretch to hold on to things.

tentacles—long, thin arms used for catching food

To Learn More

AT THE LIBRARY

Coldiron, Deborah. *Cuttlefish*. Edina, Minn.: ABDO, 2008.

Sill, Cathryn. *About Mollusks: A Guide for Children*. Atlanta, Ga.: Peachtree, 2005.

Trueit, Trudi Strain. *Octopuses, Squids, and Cuttlefish*. New York, N.Y.: Franklin Watts, 2003.

ON THE WEB

Learning more about cuttlefish is as easy as 1, 2, 3.

1. Go to www.factsurfer.com.

2. Enter "cuttlefish" into the search box.

3. Click the "Surf" button and you will see a list of related Web sites.

With factsurfer.com, finding more information is just a click away.

Index

The images in this book are reproduced through the courtesy of: James D. Watt / imagequestmarine.com, front cover, pp. 12-13; Reinhard Dirscherl / age fotostock, pp. 4-5; Marevision / age fotostock, pp. 6, 18-19; Jane Gould / Alamy, p. 7; Juniors Bildarchiv / age fotostock, pp. 8-9; Kevin Schafer / age fotostock, p. 10; Jez Tryner / imagequestmarine. com, p. 11; imagebroker / Alamy, p. 14; Peter Arnold, Inc. / Alamy, p. 15; Dray van Beeck / imagequestmarine.com, p. 16; Scott Tuason / imagequest3d.com, p. 17; Brandon Cole, p. 20; Jens Kuhfs / Getty Images, p. 21.